FAMOUS PEOPLE FAMOUS LIVES

Biographies of famous people to
support the curriculum.

Roald Dahl

by Emma Fischel
Illustrations by Martin Remphry

First published in 1999
by Franklin Watts
This edition 2002

Franklin Watts
96 Leonard Street
London EC2A 4XD

Franklin Watts Australia
56 O'Riordan Street
Alexandria, Sydney
NSW 2015

ISBN 0 7496 4351 X

A CIP catalogue record for this book is
available from the British Library

Dewey Decimal Classification
Number: 823/DAH

10 9 8 7 6 5 4 3 2 1

Series Editor: Sarah Ridley

Printed in Great Britain

Roald Dahl

Roald Dahl is one of the most famous children's writers ever.

Even children who don't like reading very much like HIS books.

Roald knew exactly what children liked to read about and how to tell a story well.

That's why his books have sold millions of copies all over the world.

Every day letters from children and their teachers poured through his letter box. He tried to answer them all.

Both Roald's parents were Norwegian but his father ran away from Norway when he was quite young. "I shall seek my fortune abroad," he said.

By the time Roald was born his father had made lots of money. It was a good thing too, as his family was rather big.

Then sad times hit the family. Roald's father and one of his sisters died within months of each other.

The family moved to a smaller
house which Roald loved. When
he was six he went to his first
school – by tricycle. There
weren't many cars on the road
back then.

There was no television either, no videos and no cinema. But there WERE sweet shops.

Roald and his family spent
exciting summers in Norway. It
took four days to get there by
train and boat.

WELCOME TO TJOME

Back at home, Roald's mother said, "Now you are nine, it's time you went away to school. English boarding schools are the best of all!"

Roald didn't think so, though.

At thirteen he went to another
school but that was even worse.
Younger boys had to be servants
to older ones.

Roald didn't get on with many of the teachers – and they didn't get on with him. He didn't like the rules and refused to bully the small boys.

He was made captain of two sports teams but that still didn't make him popular.

Not all the teachers were bad,
though.

EXHIBITION
OF
PHOTOGRAPHS
BY
ROALD DAHL

ART TEACHER
ARTHUR
NORRIS

ART
ROOM

At last school was over. "And now, to university," said his mother.

"Not likely!" said Roald. "I shall become a businessman and travel the world."

"We are sending you to Egypt," said one of his bosses two years later.

"Too dusty!" said Roald. "And I'd like some jungles, please."

In the end they sent him to East Africa.

Roald reached Africa at last.
"So much to see," he said. "So
different from home!"

Now we see faraway countries on television but in those days people only knew what other places were like from books.

While Roald was in Africa war broke out between Britain and Germany.

"I shall fly fighter planes for Britain," he said. "Once I learn how!" Then he drove six hundred miles to join the airforce.

Roald loved learning to fly. He was twenty-three …

and so tall his head stuck out of the plane.

But before he could do any
fighting he had a terrible crash.

It took him six months to
recover – and he limped for the
rest of his life.

Now he was sent to Greece to fight. But he had never flown in a battle before and he hardly knew how to fly the kind of plane they gave him.

Roald had trained with sixteen people. Thirteen of them died in the war.

After two months Roald started
to get terrible headaches. He
couldn't fly properly any more.

"It's because of that crash," said
the doctors. "You're no use
to the airforce. Go home."

Before long he was sent to America as a sort of spy. He had only been there three days when he met someone who changed his life.

"I'm writing about the war for a magazine," said the man. "Tell me about your flying days."

"I can do better than that," said Roald. "I'll write it all down for you instead."

The next thing he knew, every word he had written was printed in the magazine!

After that Roald became a
writer but his first books were
for grown-ups.

He lived some of the time in
England, some in America.

It was in America that he met a
famous actress, Patricia Neal.
They married within a year
and bought a house in England.

They had five children, four girls and a boy. Roald used to tell them bedtime stories. Later, these stories would become his first children's books.

Roald was forty-five when his
first children's book was published.
Then three years later, his second.
They sold more and more ...

IN TODAY!
JAMES AND THE
GIANT PEACH
CHARLIE AND THE
CHOCOLATE FACTORY

... and more.

Not everyone liked his books as much as children did though. Not that Roald worried too much about that.

Besides, he had a lot more story ideas in his head.

But terrible things were happening in Roald's life then. A taxi ran into his son Theo's pram when he was only four months old.

"He needs lots of operations and he may not get better," said the doctors.

"He will get better!" said Roald.

DOCTOR, WRITER AND AEROPLANE MODELLER INVENT THE WADE-DAHL-TILL VALVE

Roald invented a special gadget to help Theo's head get better. It helped other people too.

But then Olivia, his oldest daughter, died of measles. She was only seven.

Soon after Patricia, his wife, had something called a stroke. It made her very ill.

She doesn't remember my name.

"Two visits a week from us and lots of rest," said the doctors.

"No," said Roald. "People around her and lots to do!"

Roald made her try to get better every hour of the day. If he couldn't be there he made sure someone was.

In two years she was making films again.

When Roald was fifty-one he
went to Hollywood to write a
film script for an exciting action
movie in the famous James
Bond series.

Writing the James Bond film
was fun – but Roald never
really liked any of the films that
were made of his own books.

Back home Roald had a special hut tucked away in the garden. He did all his writing there.

At the start of every day he would sharpen six pencils to use. By the end of the day they would all be blunt.

He spoke every sentence aloud
to see if it worked. If it didn't he
rubbed it out.

Sometimes he got stuck on what
should happen next in the book.
And unstuck when he was doing
something quite different.

When he was sixty-six his own favourite book was published, *The BFG*. It was an exciting story all about a big friendly giant.

Quentin Blake, the illustrator, made the BFG look a lot like Roald.

By now every new book Roald
wrote was a bestseller. *The BFG*
was the first book to win Roald
a prize, though.

"A prize chosen by children,"
he said. "Thank you very
much!"

Roald's next book, *The Witches*, won his first prize from grown-ups.

He gave the prize money to a hospital for very ill children.

"I'm honoured," he said, "But the Children's Book Award means much more."

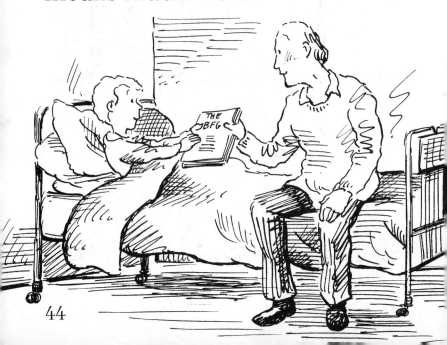

For the next six years Roald carried on writing. But he got very ill himself, with something called leukaemia.

In November 1990 he died.

More about Roald Dahl

Did you know?

Roald was an expert on lots of things – orchid-growing, fine wines and paintings. He loved antiques as well, and he and his son, Theo, opened an antique shop in 1983. They had so much furniture they were restoring for the shop that he had to drain his swimming pool so they had somewhere to put it all!

The Roald Dahl Children's Gallery

You can visit the Gallery at the Buckinghamshire County Museum in Aylesbury. See what it's really like to be inside a giant peach, try your hand on one of the amazing inventions, or come face to face with the BFG.

The Roald Dahl Foundation

Roald did a lot to help other people when he was alive. After his death the Foundation was started by Roald's second wife, Felicity. The Foundation gives help to people who have problems with reading. It also helps people with brain damage or blood diseases.

Important dates in Roald Dahl's lifetime

1916 Roald is born in Cardiff, South Wales.

1925 Roald goes to boarding school.

1930 Roald goes to Repton public school.

1938 Roald goes to Africa.

1939 War breaks out and Roald joins the RAF.

1942 Roald's first story is published in America.

1953 Roald marries Patricia Neal.

1960 Roald's son Theo's pram is hit by a taxi in New York.

1961 Roald's first children's book, *James and the Giant Peach*, is published.

1962 Olivia, Roald's oldest child, dies.

1965 Roald's wife, Patricia, has a stroke.

1967 Roald goes to Hollywood and writes a James Bond movie.

1983 Roald wins awards for *The BFG* and *The Witches*. He divorces Patricia and marries Felicity d'Abreu.

1989 Roald wins an award for *Matilda*.

1990 Roald dies.